PERFORMANCE NOTES

The format of this cantata invites the creativity of each director to adapt their presentations to meet the worship style of their congregation. The work can be presented as a musical montage alone or with a single narrator reading the scriptures provided in the vocal score. You may choose any translation that best fits your tradition.

You may wish to also include a second narrator to read the simple poem provided. I wrote this narration with a younger voice in mind. I think there is something very special about including young people in our music presentations. Their hopeful voices will be an encouragement to the congregation as they hear the work unfold.

I have also included some basic options for candle lighting and the use of symbols to enhance the visual aspects of the performance.

Feel free to substitute your own ideas for any of the suggestions I have made. I have often found the creativity of thoughtful directors and pastors far exceed any suggestions that I might make.

Let music live!

JOSEPH M. MARTIN

T0088103

Scripture for Contemplation

(This scripture may be read aloud, projected on screens or placed in the program as a reflective prelude to the cantata.)

We speak the wisdom of God, hidden in a *mystery,* that God determined before the ages for our glory. But just as it is written, "Things that no eye has seen, or ear heard, or mind imagined, are the things God has prepared for those who love Him." *(I Corinthians 2:7,9)*

Comfort, O comfort my people, says your God. Speak tenderly to Jerusalem, and cry unto her, that her warfare is accomplished, that her iniquity is pardoned; for she hath received of the LORD's hand double for all her sins.

The voice of him that cries out in the wilderness: "Prepare the way of the LORD; make straight in the desert a highway for our God. Every valley shall be lifted up, and every mountain and hill be made low; the crooked places shall be made straight, and the rough places plain. Then the glory of the LORD shall be revealed, and all people shall see it together; for the mouth of the LORD hath spoken it." *(Isaiah 40:1-5)*

… and all the people were astonished at the *majesty* of God. *(Luke 9:43)*

A CHRISTMAS FLOURISH

Words by
JOSEPH M. MARTIN
and **ISAAC WATTS** (1674-1748)

Based on tunes:
MENDELSSOHN, O SANCTISSIMA,
SOMERSET CAROL *and* **ANTIOCH**
Arranged by
JOSEPH M. MARTIN (BMI)

* Tune: MENDELSSOHN, Felix Mendelssohn (1809-1847)

32 S. *mf*

A.

*Oh, how joy-ful-ly,___ oh, how mer-ri-ly,___ Christ-mas comes with its

T. *mf*

32 B.

mf

gift of ___ grace. Light a-gain is beam-ing.

mp

Love the world re-deem-ing.

35

mp

mp

38 *mf* **3**

Tune your hearts, pre-pare the way for Christ-mas ___ day!

mf

38

mf

mp

* Tune: O SANCTISSIMA, *The European Magazine and London Review*, 1792
  Words: Joseph M. Martin
A8880

Lyrics:
Soon the world will cel - e - brate on Christ-mas___ day!

(optional solo) *Come

all ye peo - ple of the faith, give heed to what we say; re -

* Tune: SOMERSET CAROL, Traditional English Carol
  Words: Joseph M. Martin

10

call the an - cient prom - is - es of this most won-drous day. In

my - ster - y and maj - es-ty, God gives to us His grace. Let us

sing of the glo - ry, the glo - ry of the Lord.

(end. solo)

12

on earth's robes of clay. From pal - ac - es of

i - vo - ry to a sta - ble cold and gray. Let us

sing_____ of the glo - ry, the glo - ry of the

A8880

14

Oh, how joy - ful - ly,_____ oh, how mer - ri - ly,_____

let the world re - sound with joy - ful mu - sic!_____

* Tune: ANTIOCH, George Frederick Handel (1685-1759)
  Words: Isaac Watts (1674-1748)
A8880

room,____ and heav'n and na - ture__ sing, and__ heav'n and na - ture__

sing, and__ heav'n.__ and heav'n____ and na - ture

sing!

The Mystery and the Majesty
of the Ancient Prophecies

NARRATOR 1:

A shoot will rise up from the stem of Jesse; from his roots a Branch will bear fruit. The Spirit of the LORD will rest on him, the Spirit of wisdom and of understanding, the Spirit of counsel and of might, the Spirit of the knowledge and fear of the LORD. He will not judge by what he sees with his eyes, or decide by what he hears with his ears; but with righteousness he will judge the needy, with justice he will give decisions for the poor of the earth.

And in that day the wolf will live with the lamb, the leopard will lie down with the goat, the calf, the lion and the yearling together; and a little child will lead them. *(Isaiah 11:1-8)*

(The candles are lit around the open Bible. The Bible should be opened to Messianic passages from Isaiah.)

NARRATOR 2:

The mystery and the majesty
of seekers in the night,
when prophets saw through eyes of faith
the coming of the Light.

The promise of Messiah,
the covenant of grace;
O the mystery and majesty
of those amazing days.

CAROL OF LONGING

Words and music by
JOSEPH M. MARTIN (BMI)
Incorporating tune:
CAROL OF THE BIRDS

* Tune: CAROL OF THE BIRDS, Traditional French Carol

A8880

20

hearts as one. Come to us now Prom - ised Son.

Prom - ised Son.

SOPRANO
ALTO

Our hearts are like a cra - dle,

wait - ing for a child. Our lives are like a can - dle,

long - ing for a fire. Si - lence now sur-rounds us.

When will an - gels sing? A thou-sand tears have fal - len.

(end solo)

When will we see the King?

22

When will night be done? A thou-sand tears have fal - len.

When will Mes-si - ah come? The

sor-rows of our long-ing will one day pass a - way. Our

Oo

eyes will see the prom-ise come true up-on that day. Our

Oo

cries will turn to sing-ing Our tears to streams of life. The

Al - le - lu - ia!

dark of night will van-ish, re-deemed by per - fect

thou - sand tears of grate - ful joy we will greet_ the King_____ of

kings!_____ Ah!_____ We will greet the

King of kings!_____

The Mystery and the Majesty
of God's Promises

NARRATOR 1:

The wilderness and the solitary place shall be glad for them; and the desert shall rejoice, and blossom as the rose. It shall flower abundantly, and rejoice even with joy and singing. They shall see the glory of the LORD, and the majesty of our God. Then the eyes of the blind shall be opened, and the ears of the deaf shall be unstopped. Then shall the lame leap as a deer, and the tongue of the speechless sing; for in the wilderness shall waters break out, and streams in the desert. And the ransomed of the LORD shall return, and come to Zion with songs and everlasting joy upon their heads. They shall obtain joy and gladness, and sorrow and sighing shall flee away. *(Isaiah 35:1,5,6,10)*

(The advent candles are lit as the simple poem is read.)

NARRATOR 2:

The mystery and the majesty
of wonders from above,
when heaven lends its glory
and sends the gift of love.

Awake, the dawn is breaking.
Could this be the day?
Jesus soon is coming.
Rejoice! Prepare the way!

ADVENT JUBILATION

Words and music by
JOSEPH M. MARTIN (BMI)

People, rise and shine, your light has

Music copyright © 2000 Malcolm Music, Words copyright © 2009 Malcolm Music
(A Division of Shawnee Press, Inc., Nashville, TN 37212)
International Copyright Secured. All Rights Reserved.

A8880

36

The Mystery and the Majesty
of the Annunciation

NARRATOR 1:

In the sixth month, God sent the angel Gabriel to Nazareth, a town in Galilee, to a virgin pledged to be married to a man named Joseph, a descendant of David. The virgin's name was Mary. The angel went to her and said, "Greetings, you who are highly favored! The Lord is with you."

Mary was greatly troubled at his words and wondered what kind of greeting this might be. But the angel said to her, "Do not be afraid, Mary, you have found favor with God. You will be with child and give birth to a son, and you are to give him the name Jesus. He will be great and will be called the Son of the Most High. The Lord God will give Him the throne of his father David, and he will reign over the house of Jacob forever; his kingdom will never end." *(Luke 1:26-33)*

(A rose is brought and placed on the altar.)

NARRATOR 2:

O the mystery and the majesty
of miracles and signs,
when Gabriel, the messenger,
brought news of the divine.

Lift up your eyes to heaven.
Wipe away your tears,
for Mary's son is coming.
His birth is drawing near.

THE COMING JOY

Words by
JOSEPH M. MARTIN

Based on tunes:
DING! DONG! MERRILY ON HIGH
and **GOOD KING WENCESLAS**
Arranged by
JOSEPH M. MARTIN (BMI)

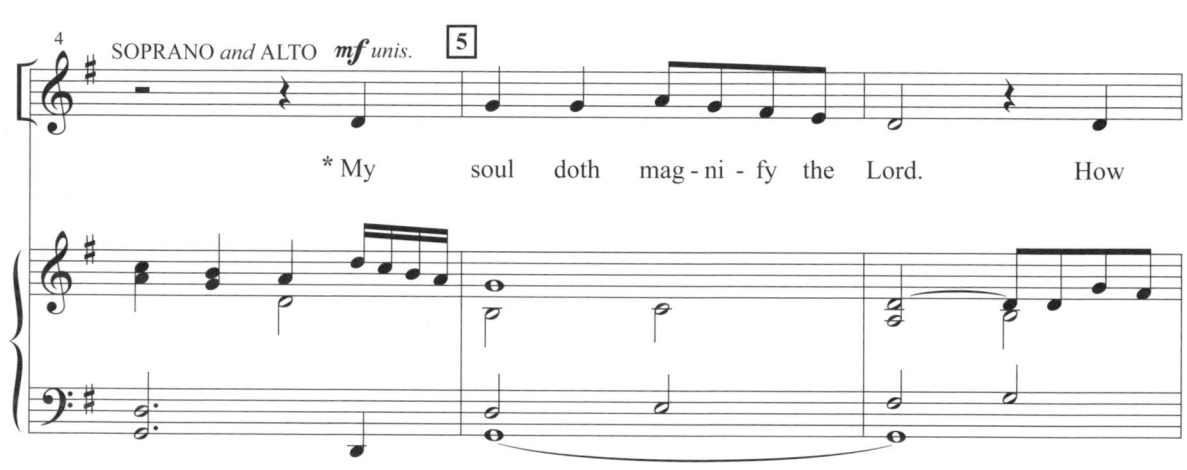

* Tune: DING! DONG! MERRILY ON HIGH, Traditional French Carol

A8880

san - na_ in_ ex - cel - sis.

SOPRANO

ALTO

My soul doth mag-ni-fy the Lord, for

God has shown me fa - vor. Soon I'll greet the hap-py

44

san - na___ in___ ex - cel - sis.

smoothly with expression

*Gen - tle Ma - ry, cho - sen one, hear this sal - u -

* Tune: GOOD KING WENCESLAS, Traditional Swedish Carol

prom - ised King__ of Is - ra - el, bring - ing joy un -

end - ing.

My

The Mystery and the Majesty
of Immanuel (God With Us)

NARRATOR 1:

In those days Caesar Augustus issued a decree that a census should be taken of the entire Roman world… and everyone went to his own town to register.

So Joseph went up from the town of Nazareth in Galilee to Judea, even unto Bethlehem the town of David, because he belonged to the house and line of David. He went there to register with Mary, who was pledged to be married to him and was expecting a child. While they were there, the time came for the baby to be born, and she gave birth to her firstborn, a son. She wrapped him in cloths and placed him in a manger, because there was no room for them in the inn. *(Luke 2:1,3-7)*

(The Christ candle is lit.)

NARRATOR 2:

O the mystery and the majesty
of Christ Immanuel,
as the Maker of the Universe
with His creation dwells.

From palaces of ivory
to a stable cold and gray;
O the mystery and majesty
of this most sacred day.

UPON A MIDNIGHT CLEAR

Based on tunes:
CAROL,
THE COVENTRY CAROL
and **O JESULEIN SÜSS! O JESULEIN MILD!**
Arranged by
JOSEPH M. MARTIN (BMI)

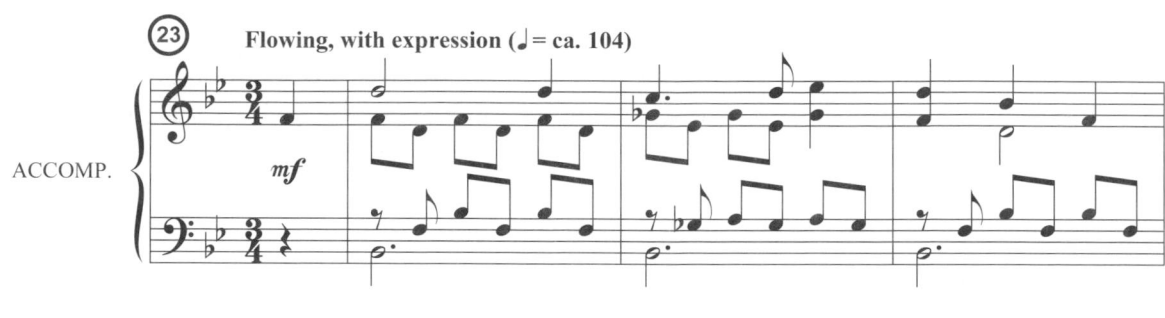

* Tune: CAROL, Richard Storrs Willis (1819-1900)
Words: Edmund H. Sears (1810-1876)

A8880

53

A8880

54

all, from heav - en's gra - cious King." The

world in sol - emn still - ness lay, to

hear the an - gels sing.

* Lul - ly, lul - lay, Thou lit-tle ti - ny child.

* Tune: THE COVENTRY CAROL, English melody
  Words: Attributed to Robert Croo (1534), new words by Joseph M. Martin
A8880

56

A8880

58

A8880

60

* Tune: O JESULEIN SÜSS! O JESULEIN MILD!, German carol
Words: Georg Christian Schemelli (1676-1762), new words by Joseph M. Martin

A8880

down, and laid a - side Your star - ry crown. O Je - sus sweet, O Je - sus mild. One day cre - a - tion shall

The Mystery and the Majesty
of Angelic Acclamation

NARRATOR 1:

And there were shepherds living out in the fields nearby, keeping watch over their flocks at night. An angel of the Lord appeared to them, and the glory of the Lord shone around them, and they were terrified.

But the angel said to them, "Do not be afraid. I bring you good news of great joy that will be for all the people. Today in the town of David a Savior has been born to you; He is Christ the Lord. This will be a sign to you: You will find a baby wrapped in cloths and lying in a manger."

Suddenly, a great company of the heavenly host appeared with the angel, praising God and saying, "Glory to God in the highest, and on earth peace to all on whom his favor rests." *(Luke 2:8-14)*

(The angel icon is illuminated.)

NARRATOR 2:

O the mystery and the majesty
of angels in the sky,
declaring peace to all the world
and glory to God on high.

The hills ring out with joyful song.
The valleys echo praise.
O the mystery and the majesty
of the Father's dazzling ways.

A CALL TO CHRISTMAS JOY *

Words by
J. PAUL WILLIAMS (ASCAP)

Music by
JON PAIGE (BMI)
and JOSEPH M. MARTIN (BMI)

* Octavo available separately – A7586
** Optional voicing through m. 13: Basses alone on bottom staff, Tenors sing the Alto part, Altos sing the Soprano II part.

A8880

Glo - ri - a, glo - ri - a, glo - ri - a, glo - ry to God.

Come, sing un - to the Lord a ju - bi - lant song.

Come, sing un - to the Lord with

Glo - ri - a in__ ex - cel - sis De - o.

* Words: anonymous, taken from French Carol, "Angels We Have Heard on High"

* Tune: IN DULCI JUBILO, 14th century German carol
  Words: medieval Latin carol; tr. John M. Neale (1818-1866), alt.

A8880

70

A8880

day._____ Christ is born to-day.

Let all cre - a - tion re - joice and sing.

Let the al - le - lu - ias ring, giv - ing praise___ to

cresc. poco a poco

Christ the King. Glo - ri - a, glo - ri - a, glo - ri - a, glo - ry to God in the high - est! Glo - ry to God! Give all glo - ry to God!

The Mystery and the Majesty
of the Adoration of the Magi

NARRATOR 1:

After Jesus was born in Bethlehem in Judea, during the time of King Herod, Magi from the east came to Jerusalem and asked, "Where is the one who has been born king of the Jews? We saw His star in the east and have come to worship Him."

When King Herod heard this, he was disturbed, and all Jerusalem with him. When he had called together all the people's chief priests and teachers of the law, he asked them where the Christ was to be born. "In Bethlehem in Judea," they replied, for this is what the prophet has written:

But you, Bethlehem, in the land of Judah, are by no means least among the rulers of Judah; for out of you will come a ruler who will be the shepherd of my people Israel. *(Matthew 2:1-6)*

(The Gifts of the Magi are brought forward to the altar, or an offering may be taken for the poor and brought to the altar.)

NARRATOR 2:

O the mystery and the majesty
of Jesus' holy birth,
when the Shepherd of the shining stars
became a Lamb on earth.

From the golden streets of heaven
to a bed of golden hay;
O the mystery and the majesty
of this most wondrous day.

JOURNEY TO BETHLEHEM

Based on tunes:
**CHILDREN'S SONG OF THE NATIVITY,
CRADLE SONG** *and* **STILLE NACHT**
Arranged by
JOSEPH M. MARTIN (BMI)

* Tune: CHILDREN'S SONG OF THE NATIVITY, English Folk Tune
Words: Frances Chesterton (1875-1938)

A8880

star? Can we see the Christ child, is He with -

in? If we lift the wood-en latch, may we go

in?

TENOR

BASS

*Oh,

mp *unis.*

* Words: Joseph M. Martin
A8880

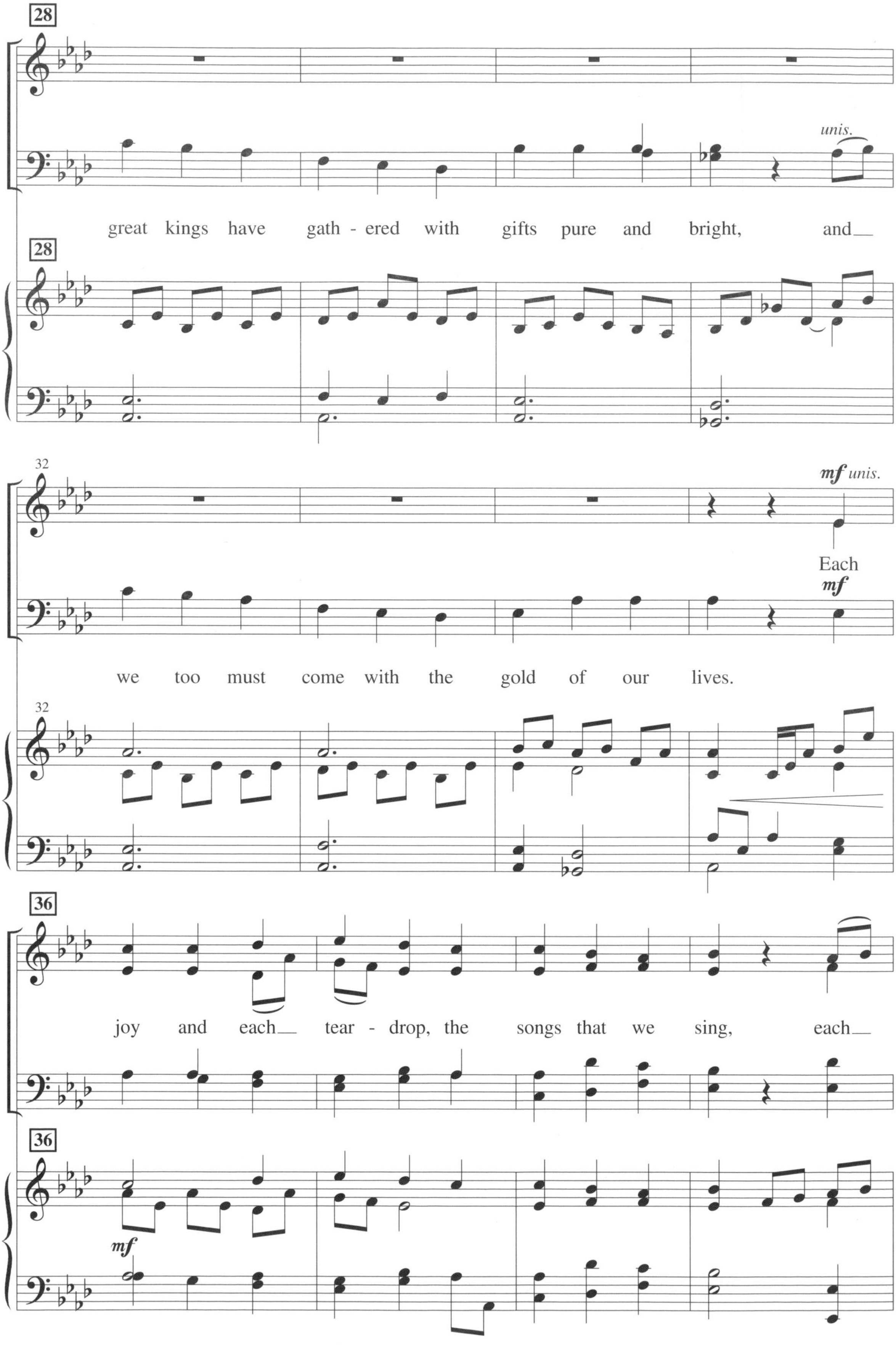
28
unis.
great kings have gath - ered with gifts pure and bright, and
28
32
mf unis.
Each
mf
we too must come with the gold of our lives.
32
36
joy and each tear - drop, the songs that we sing, each
36
mf

bur - den and sor - row, the gifts that we bring.

SOLO

poco rit. mp

* Be

near me, Lord Je - sus, I ask You to stay close

With freedom (♩ = ca. 69)

S.
A.
Oo
T.
B.

* Tune: CRADLE SONG, William J. Kirkpatrick (1838-1921)
Words: Anonymous, alt.
A8880

by me for - ev - er and_ love me, I pray. Bless

all of Your_ peo - ple with_ Your ten - der care, and_

take us to heav - en to__ live with You

Oo__ to__

live with You there._____ How_ far is it to

* Tune: STILLE NACHT, Franz Gruber (1787-1863)
  Words: Joseph Mohr (1792-1848)

A8880

The Mystery and the Majesty
of the Incarnation

NARRATOR 1:

…and now this is the mystery and majesty of the incarnation:

In the beginning was the Word, and the Word was with God, and the Word was God. He was with God in the beginning. Through Him all things were made; without Him nothing was made that has been made. In Him was life, and that life was the light of all people. *(John 1:1-5)*

(The altar and chancel candles are illuminated.)

NARRATOR 2:

O the mystery and the majesty
of all that God has done,
when the ancient of Days
became a newborn Son.

How the King of heaven
put on earth's robes of clay;
O the mystery and the majesty
of this most wondrous day.

THE BEAUTIFUL IMPOSSIBLE

Words and music by
JOSEPH M. MARTIN (BMI)

A8880

earth, the mys-ter-y and maj-es-ty of a mir-a-cle na-tiv-i-ty, the beau-ti-ful im-pos-si-ble, Je-sus is born.

(end solo)

84

A8880

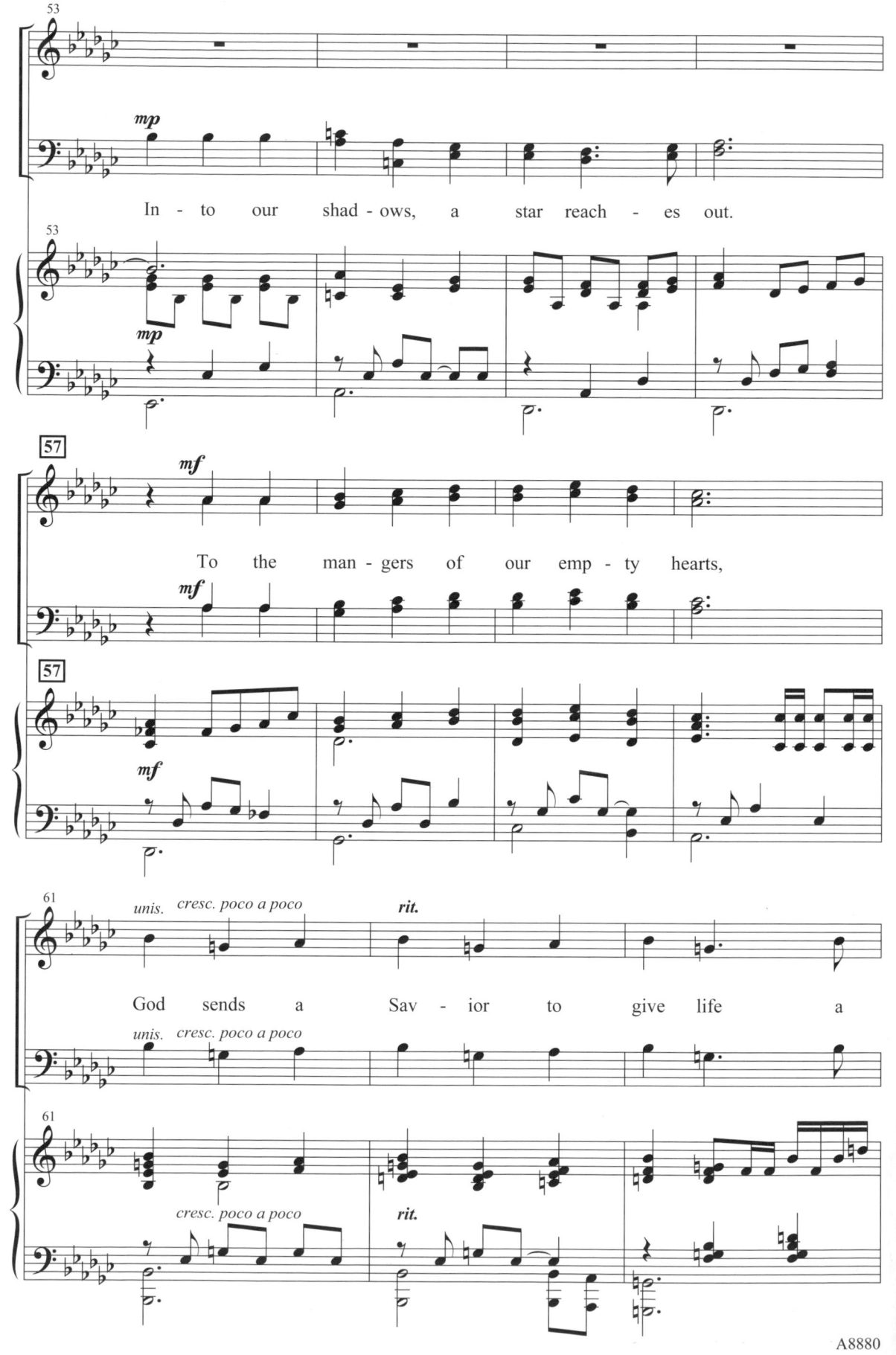

Into our shad - ows, a star reach - es out.

To the man - gers of our emp - ty hearts,

God sends a Sav - ior to give life a

The Mystery and the Majesty
of Christmas

NARRATOR 1:

For to us a child is born, to us a son is given, and the government will be on His shoulders. And He will be called Wonderful Counselor, Mighty God, Everlasting Father, and the Prince of Peace. *(Isaiah 9:6)*

(The remaining candles are lit in the sanctuary as the light symbolically goes forth into the world)

NARRATOR 2:

O the mystery and the majesty
of all this season brings:
the joy and hope that thrill the heart,
the wonders of the King of kings.

Now let us all declare the news.
Lift high the angel song,
and celebrate the miracle
of Christmas all year long.

A NOEL PROCLAMATION

Based on tunes:
REGENT SQUARE, MARGARET,
WALTHAM, ADESTE FIDELES
and **THE FIRST NOWELL**
Arranged by
JOSEPH M. MARTIN (BMI)

Come and wor-ship. Wor-ship Christ_ the_ new-born King.

Come and wor-ship. Come and wor-ship. Wor-ship Christ_ the_

new - born King. *Thou didst

mf unis.

poco rit.

* Tune: MARGARET, Timothy R. Matthews (1826-1910)
  Words: Emily E. S. Elliot (1836-1897)
A8880

94

Je - sus. There is room in my heart for Thee.

* I

heard the bells on Christ - mas day, their old fa - mil - iar

* Tune: WALTHAM, John Calkin (1827-1905)
  Words: Henry W. Longfellow (1807-1882)

A8880

world re - volved from night to day, a voice, a chime, a

chant sub - lime, of peace on earth, good - will_____ to_____

men!

* Tune: ADESTE FIDELES, John Francis Wade (1710-1786)
  Words: John Francis Wade (1710-1786)

A8880

Christ the Lord.

*The

first No - el the an - gel did say, was to

* Tune: THE FIRST NOWELL, Taditional English Carol
  Words: Traditional English Carol
A8880

certain poor shepherds in fields where they lay; in fields where they lay, keeping their sheep, on a cold winter's night that was so deep. No-

el,_____ No - el, No - el,_____ No - el,_____

born is the King_____ of Is - ra - el.

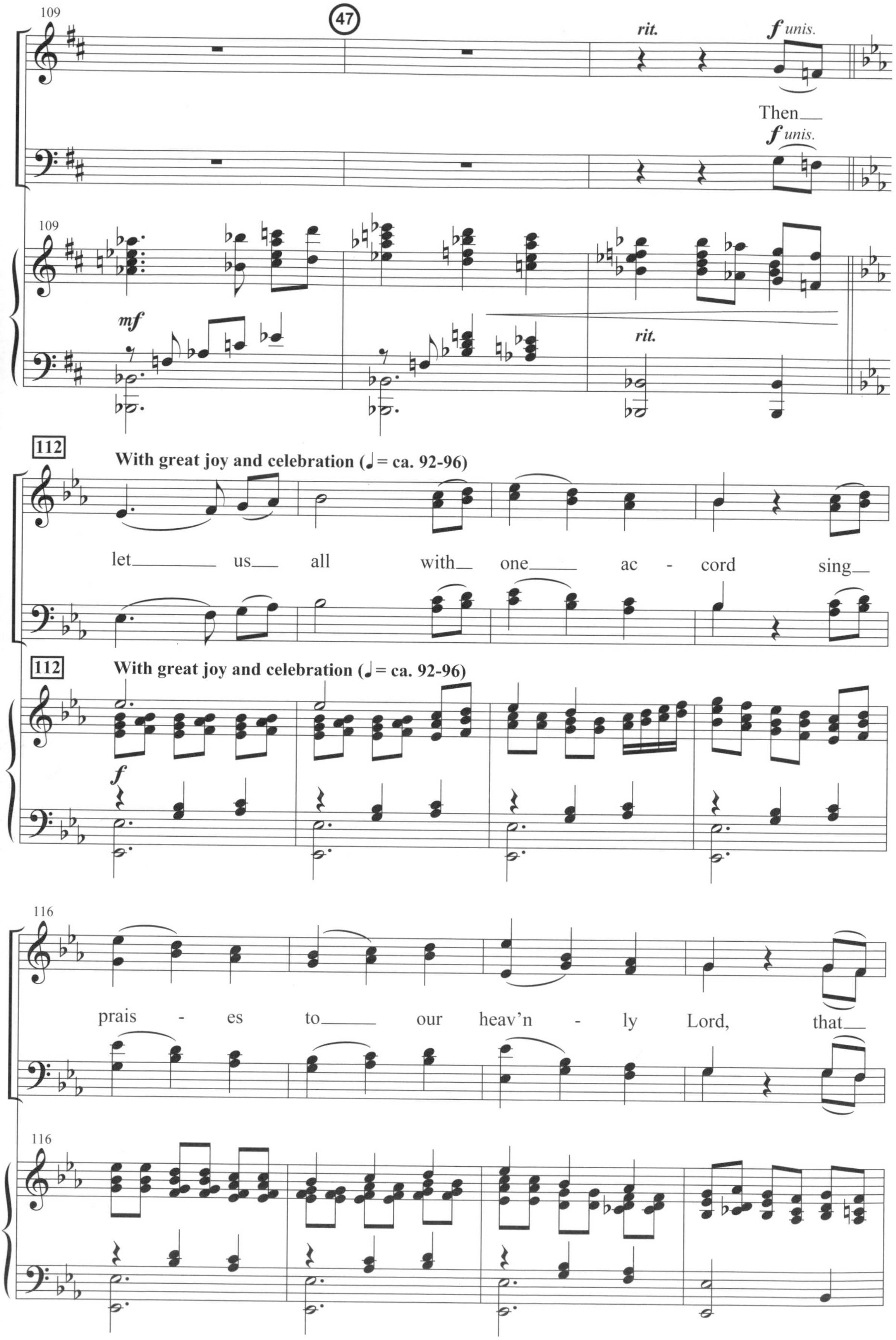
109
47
rit.
f unis.
Then
f unis.
109
mf
rit.
112
With great joy and celebration (♩ = ca. 92-96)
let us all with one ac - cord sing
112
With great joy and celebration (♩ = ca. 92-96)
f
116
prais - es to our heav'n - ly Lord, that
116

hath____ made____ heav'n and____ earth____ of____ naught, and____ with____ His blood____ man - kind____ hath bought.____ No -

INTRODUCING...

A8880 $8.95

the MYSTERY *and the* MAJESTY

A Cantata by Joseph M. Martin

Harold Flammer
MUSIC
A Division of Shawnee Press, Inc.
Nashville, TN 37212

DIGITAL RESOURCE KIT

Here's a great new resource that will enhance and enrich your preparation and presentation of THE MYSTERY AND THE MAJESTY. The "Digital Resource Kit" contains materials designed to make this an unforgettable worship experience for your entire church and community.

CD-ROM containing PowerPoint
(These PowerPoint presentations will help visually segue your audience between musical movements)
Reproducible Posters *(Full-color artwork to help spread the word about your presentation)*
Programs *(Full-color cover with blank 3-sided template)*
Biographical Information *(Information about the composer your choir will enjoy knowing)*
Rehearsal Tips & Choir Devotionals *(Written by Lee & Susan Dengler, these are designed to maximize your rehearsal time and enrich the spiritual experience for you and your choir)*
Real-Time Audio Commentary by Joseph M. Martin
(A unique feature which leads the director through the entire cantata with comments and tips about presenting the work)
Children's Bulletin *(Containing coloring pages and games for youngest members of congregation)*

DRK5001
Available from your favorite music retailer.

Shawnee Press, Inc.